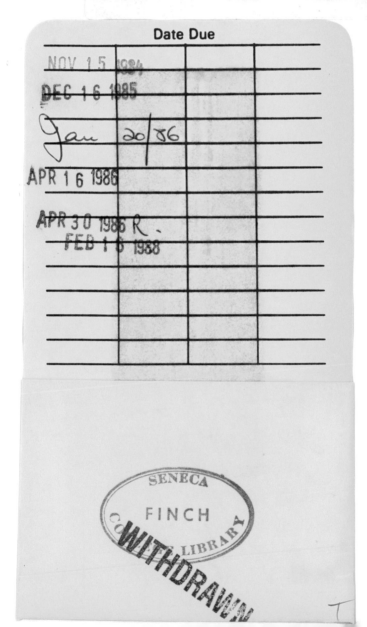

Sainte-Carmen of the Main

Sainte-Carmen of the Main

a play by
Michel Tremblay

translated by
John Van Burek

Talonbooks
Vancouver

1981

copyright © 1976 Les Editions Leméac Inc.
translation copyright © 1981 John Van Burek

published with assistance from the Canada Council

Talonbooks
201 1019 East Cordova
Vancouver
British Columbia V6A 1M8
Canada

This book was typeset by Rosaire MacNeil, designed by
David Robinson and printed in Canada by Hignell for
Talonbooks.

First printing: October 1981

Rights to produce *Sainte-Carmen of the Main,* in whole or in part,
in any medium by any group, amateur or professional, are
retained by the author and interested persons are requested to
apply to his agent, John Goodwin, 4235, avenue de
l'Esplanade, Montréal, Québec H2W 1T1

First published by Les Editions Leméac Inc., Montréal,
Québec. Published by arrangement with Les Editions
Leméac Inc.

Canadian Cataloguing in Publication Data

Tremblay, Michel, 1942 —
    (Sainte-Carmen de la Main. English)
    Sainte-Carmen of the Main

    Translation of: Sainte-Carmen de la Main.
    ISBN 0-88922-181-2

    I. Title.   II. Title: Sainte-Carmen de la Main. English.
PS8539.R47S313   C842'.54   C81-091342-9
PQ3919.2.T73S313

Sainte-Carmen de la Main was first performed by la Compagnie Jean Duceppe at Théâtre Maisonneuve in Montréal, Québec on July 20, 1976, with the following cast:

Carmen	Michelle Rossignol
Gloria	Carmen Tremblay
Harelip	Amulette Garneau
Maurice	Denis Drouin
Toothpick	Marc Legault
Sandra	Normand Lévesque
Rose Beef	Louise Saint-Pierre
Chorus	Normand Morin, Hubert Gagnon, Louis Amiot, René Gagnon, Michel-René Labelle, René-Daniel Dubois, Lorraine Pintal, Pauline Lapointe, Anne Caron, Murielle Dutil, Paule Marier, Suzanne Marier.

Directed by André Brassard
Set Design by Guy Nepveau
Costume Design by François Laplante
Lighting Design and Sound by Michel Beaulieu

Sainte-Carmen of the Main was first performed in English at Tarragon Theatre in Toronto, Ontario on January 14, 1978, with the following cast:

Carmen	Brenda Donohue
Gloria	Helen Hughes
Harelip	Clare Coulter
Maurice	Ken James
Toothpick	Ray Whelan
Sandra	Robert Benson
Rose Beef	Frances Fagan
Chorus	Bob Baker, Michael J. Evans, Richard Macmillan, Angelo Pedari, Diane Douglass, Margaret Dragu, Jan Kudelka, Rhonda Kristi.

Directed by André Brassard
Set and Costume Design by Meredith Caron
Lighting Design by Bill Williams

Act One

*Two CHORUSES enter slowly, the first led by
SANDRA; the second by ROSE BEEF.*

CHORUS I:
> This morning the sun came up.

CHORUS II:
> This morning.

CHORUS I:
> The sun.

CHORUS II:
> I saw it.

CHORUS I AND II:
> I saw the sun come up this morning at the end of la rue
> Ste-Catherine.

CHORUS I:
> A big ball of red fire.

CHORUS II:
> Blood.

CHORUS I AND II:
> Blood red.

SANRDA:

> Usually the sun keeps me waiting....

ROSE BEEF:

> It's late coming up, usually....

SANDRA AND ROSE BEEF:

> I have to keep looking down the end of the street to see a difference in the sky....

SANDRA:

> But this morning it came up...

CHORUS I AND II:

> ...all of a sudden!

ROSE BEEF:

> There was no change in the sky....

SANDRA:

> It was dark, then all of a sudden....

CHORUS I AND II:

> The sun came into the world like a red fist at the end of la Catherine.

SANDRA:

> It was beautiful!

ROSE BEEF:

> It was beautiful!

CHORUS I: I stayed on my side of the street....
CHORUS II: I stayed on my side of the street....

CHORUS I: I just yelled at the girls
CHORUS II: I just yelled

CHORUS I: on the other side:
CHORUS II:

CHORUS I AND II:
Aie, did you see that? Two minutes ago, it wasn't there!
Now look! Look how it came up fast this morning!

SANDRA AND ROSE BEEF:
I leaned against my store window...and I watched....
It's almost as if...I heard it!

CHORUS I AND II: *softly*
As if it were the very first time!

SANDRA:
No way I was going to bed....

ROSE BEEF:
No.

SANDRA AND ROSE BEEF:
I didn't want to now!

CHORUS I: Though I'd been talking about it all night
CHORUS II: all night

CHORUS I:
CHORUS II: as usual.

SANDRA:
I was complaining all night long.

ROSE BEEF:
My feet were killing me...

SANDRA:
It was cold....

ROSE BEEF:
...there were no customers....

SANDRA:
The pigs came by more often...

ROSE BEEF:
> . . . they oinked a lot more. . . .

SANDRA:
> My feet were killing me . . .

ROSE BEEF:
> . . . it was cold . . .

SANDRA:
> . . . no customers. . . .

ROSE BEEF:
> I started talking about going home at three . . .

SANDRA:
> . . . right after closing.

ROSE BEEF:
> . . . but the girls told me:

CHORUS II:
> Wait a little. . . .

CHORUS I:
> It's early yet. . . .

CHORUS II:
> Wait a little longer!

CHORUS I:
> You gotta do your night!

CHORUS I AND II:
> So I hung around. But I didn't score. Stayed up all night for nothing.

SANDRA:
> No, that's not true.

ROSE BEEF:
>   I didn't stay up for nothing. That's not true.

CHORUS I AND II:
>   'Cause this morning for the first time, the sun rose over
>   la Catherine.

CHORUS I:
>   And I saw it!

CHORUS II:
>   And I heard it!

CHORUS I AND II:
>   Ah! It exploded without warning, and I stood frozen to
>   the corner of the Main . . . with tears in my eyes.

ROSE BEEF:
>   Like a flash, it came clear in my head.

SANDRA:
>   I jumped three feet in the air, I started yelling at the
>   girls.

SANDRA AND ROSE BEEF:
>   I know why!

CHORUS I AND II:
>   I know why the sun rose like that this morning! It's for
>   Carmen!

CHORUS I: It's for Carmen!
CHORUS II: It's for Carmen!
SANDRA: It's for Carmen!
ROSE BEEF: It's for Carmen!

CHORUS I AND II:
>   Today's the day Carmen comes back, and the sun's
>   decided to celebrate!

SANDRA:

It came up earlier!

ROSE BEEF:

It came up faster!

CHORUS I AND II:

It'll be a long day! It'll be a long day because tonight Carmen comes home!

SANDRA:

We ran out and kissed each other in the middle of the street. We smacked one another on the ass.

ROSE BEEF:

Today is a holiday! No one on the Main went to bed. All day long the queens chirped like birds in a cage.

SANDRA:

The pimps are all spiffed up!

ROSE BEEF:

I spent a whole hour in the bath, just thinking about her.

SANDRA:

Me, I got out my best wig. The one that's three feet high and gives everyone the shits.

CHORUS I AND II:

Today la Catherine got a facelift and the Main has been washed. Carmen is back!

SANDRA:

I saw her this afternoon.

ROSE BEEF:

She was going into the Rodéo when I passed by.

SANDRA: She was _so_ beautiful...Even without her
ROSE BEEF: I didn't dare go in....I didn't dare!

SANDRA: costume, she shone like the sun!
ROSE BEEF:

CHORUS I:
    The sun!

SANDRA AND ROSE BEEF:
    The sun!

CHORUS II:
    The sun!

CHORUS I AND II:
    The sun is Carmen!

SANDRA:
    It's Carmen who rose this morning over la Catherine!

ROSE BEEF:
    It's Carmen who warmed the Main all afternoon!

CHORUS I AND II:
    It's Carmen who's high above me and watches over me!

SANDRA: Carmen, it's me,

ROSE BEEF: You haven't forgotten me, Carmen, it's me,
SANDRA: Sandra!

ROSE BEEF: Rose Beef!

A tired orchestra is heard launching into some Country and
Western song.

SANDRA AND ROSE BEEF:
    No, you haven't forgotten me....

CHORUS I AND II:

>It's for me that you've come back, Carmen!

CHORUS I:

>The West End of the city has been cloudy all day.

CHORUS II:

>It's just us who've got the sun.

CHORUS I AND II:

>And tonight, the sun won't set in the west, either.

CHORUS I:

>No, it will disappear behind the clouds, beyond the Main....

ROSE BEEF:

>To get into costume!

CHORUS I AND II:

>Because tonight, the sun comes back to sing for us!
>Tonight, the sun comes home to sing...for me.

>*The orchestra stops. Slowly, CARMEN enters, followed
>by HARELIP. CARMEN is all dressed for her show,
>but still a few last minute details to her costume have to be
>attended to; the cowgirl hat, the gloves, the belt. During
>CARMEN's speech, HARELIP will help her with these,
>much the way a choirboy would help a priest with his final
>ornaments before an important ceremony.*

CARMEN:

>I haven't sat still for the past two months, Harelip. I
>knew I was ready. I was more restless than a mare in
>her stall.... My songs were ready.... And I knew you
>were all waiting for me back here. Hey, Harelip, do you
>know I translated the songs from English myself? I can
>do it now! Tonight, I'll be singing my own words! You
>should have seen them in Nashville.... They kept
>asking me: "You sure you can translate that into
>French, yourself?" "I don't know if it'll be French," I told

them, "but don't worry, they'll understand me back home!" And my translations are good too! Harelip, I know what these songs mean, like I'd written them myself. They're my songs now 'cause I've worked on them. I practiced for six months, Harelip, with real musicians. . . . I mean, *real* ones. Those guys sure know their music. And they taught me a lot. . . . Every day, I'd say to myself: "Wait till the Main hears this! They haven't heard a thing! My present to them will be the most beautiful Country and Western recital they've ever heard!" Last week, when Maurice showed up with a new car, I knew right then it was time to come home. I laughed! And I sang for Maurice. You should have seen him! His jaw dropped to the floor. . . . If you only knew how I've changed in six months. I've got this new song, Harelip, and when I start yodelling at the end, it's like it's not even me who's singing any more. I feel like someone bigger, stronger . . . who's soaring and who's looking down as she rides the wind. . . . Music is like the wind, Harelip. . . . You've gotta learn to ride it, learn to use it. Conquer it. And once you've got it . . . you're no longer the same. Maurice was crying when I finished! Can you believe it? Maurice? He took me in his arms and called me his baby, his little girl. . . . You know, it's because of him, your brother, that I could go . . . study in the States. . . . And that, I'll never forget. Even when I make it to the top!

> *TOOTHPICK appears. He comes and stands a few feet away from CARMEN and HARELIP.*

What's he doing here? I said I didn't want to see him again! How come he's still here? I said I wanted him gone before I came back!

TOOTHPICK:
I told you, Carmen, if you come back, I'll have your ass. You've come back. I'll find a way.

*CARMEN exits. For a moment, TOOTHPICK stands
in the centre of the stage, victorious, then he goes off.
HARELIP is left standing alone.*

HARELIP:

They say that when Carmen came into the world, her
mother, Marie-Louise, who didn't know how children
were born, screamed in her bed: "Don't let them rip my
navel. I don't want them to rip my navel." And when
the doctor had explained that children aren't born
through the navel and he'd told her how they are born,
they say that Marie-Louise stood up beside her bed,
right in the middle of labour, screaming: "That's even
worse! If that's where babies come from, then babies are
dirty! I don't want any!" They had to knock Marie-
Louise out so Carmen could be born. That's what
they say. That happened during the war. Carmen told
me herself. She heard it from her father, Léopold, who
used to tell it at family gatherings when he was drunk.
They say that when Marie-Louise woke up after the
delivery, all she could say was: "If it's mother's cunt is
the first thing a child ever sees, it's no wonder we're all
in the shit." And she refused to see her baby. For a year.
That's what they say.

SANDRA and ROSE BEEF enter.

SANDRA:
Did you see her?

HARELIP:
Huh?

ROSE BEEF:
Her! Did you see her?

HARELIP:
Who, "her?"...Carmen?

SANDRA:
Yes, Carmen!

HARELIP:

> Yes, I just finished dressing her.

ROSE BEEF:

> Already?

HARELIP:

> She wants to practice in costume.

ROSE BEEF:

> Is she practicing now?

HARELIP:

> Yes.

SANDRA:

> Can I go in?

HARELIP:

> No.

ROSE BEEF:

> I'd love to see her.

HARELIP:

> I said no. Nobody sees Carmen in costume before tonight.

SANDRA AND ROSE BEEF:

> Is she beautiful?

HARELIP:

> Beautiful? Oh, yes!

SANDRA AND ROSE BEEF:

> More than before?

HARELIP:

> More than before.

She approaches SANDRA and ROSE BEEF.

HARELIP:
> Her skin...her skin is softer than before. Whiter. And she's thinner. But not too thin. She was just a bit fat when she left, but now...she's perfect! Her legs are firmer. Her arms more beautiful. She's white as a dove. Her eyes...you'd think her eyes have gotten bigger. She stands taller than before. When she comes near you...you feel like you're nothing. All you want to do is adore her.... But she's as nice as ever, though. No nicer than before.... She could never be nicer than she was...that'd be impossible.

SANDRA:
> Her new costume...

HARELIP:
> Ah!

ROSE BEEF:
> Is it...

SANDRA AND ROSE BEEF:
> ...like the sun?

HARELIP:
> How did you know?

SANDRA:
> Have you heard her sing?

HARELIP:
> No.

ROSE BEEF:
> I hear she's written all new songs.

HARELIP:
> That's what she told me.

SANDRA:
> But she'll still sing the old hits....

18

HARELIP:
Probably. She didn't say.

SANDRA AND ROSE BEEF:
The word's out that...tonight...will be a big night.

HARELIP:
Yes. Tonight will be a big night!

HARELIP, SANDRA AND ROSE BEEF:
It's like I'm preparing to die from love!

CHORUS I AND II:
The neon lights are lit. The Main is empty. All is quiet. Night falls as fast as the day began. Greta-the-Old crosses la Catherine as fast as she can; she goes into the five-and-dime. Her best set of nails has disappeared. Meanshile, Greta-the-Young is blowing on her Cutex, her spidery fingers spread wide. Bambi can't get her second eye to match the first. She curses. I saw Hosanna in her window. Hosanna won't come tonight, she's too proud. But she'll spend the whole evening with her nose glued to the pane. Betty Bird has closed her pigsty. Purple has bought a new pair of stockings. Catherine the Great depilates. Big Pauline-de-Joliette just tried her new platform shoes, the ones with the six-inch soles. Tonight, Big Pauline-de-Joliette will be seven feet tall. Sandra and Rose Beef are pacing outside the club. We're going to miss La Duchesse de Langeais. La Duchesse de Langeais is dead. She was murdered in a parking lot two weeks ago.

CARMEN and MAURICE enter.

MAURICE:
Why get so worked up? Christ, Toothpick's only Toothpick.

CARMEN:
I hate his guts, can't you understand that?

MAURICE:

> No, as a matter of fact, I can't.

CARMEN:

> Maurice, Toothpick is the only one on the Main who
> gives me shit and I won't stand for it. The last week I
> sang here, he came every night, he sat right in front and
> he laughed. He laughed at me the whole week,
> Maurice! He bothered everyone, talking out loud,
> spilling his drinks, whatever he could to mess me up. It
> was so bad even the customers were telling him to shut
> up. I don't want him to start again, Maurice, not
> tonight. I didn't spend six months training in the States
> to be laughed at by some punk on the Main.

MAURICE:

> Okay, I'll tell him . . . .

CARMEN:

> I don't want you to tell him, I want you to squash him.
> I want him to disappear. Hell, he wouldn't be the first
> one! Pay him or kill him, but do something!

MAURICE:

> Relax! You're excited tonight and you don't know what
> you're saying . . . .

CARMEN:

> I know damn well what I'm saying. I want you to shut
> him up like you shut up Dum-Dum four years ago,
> okay? Why didn't you do something to keep him from
> laughing six months ago? Why didn't you do something
> to get rid of him while I was gone? And why do I find
> him here in my dressing room when I'm getting dressed
> this afternoon? Are you scared of him? Eh? Is there
> something stopping you that I don't know about?

MAURICE:

> Toothpick doesn't scare me! Nobody scares me!

CARMEN:

Come off it, Maurice! Maybe people around here need
you, but you need them too. Everybody's scared of you
'cause you can hurt them, but there are times I wonder
if they don't scare you for the same reason. Like me, for
instance. If I decided to split for good and if I went and
blabbed everything I know to you know who, wouldn't
you be scared, Maurice?

MAURICE:

You wouldn't do that.

CARMEN:

That's not the point. Your web is badly spun, Maurice,
and one of these days the spider might choke to death in
the midst of his flies. You know, sometimes I watch you
sleep, and believe me, you're not always beautiful.
Maurice, the Main and la Catherine ought to be scared
shitless of you. You should lord it over them like a rat
on a stiff in the garbage. At times, I think the Main got
stuck with a second-hand king.

MAURICE:

I don't know why you drag all that up again, now, an
an hour before your show. . . .

CARMEN:

Toothpick is a shitfly, Maurice, and shitflies carry
disease. . . . I'm right, aren't I, you're scared of him?

MAURICE:

I'm not scared of him as long as he's with me.

CARMEN:

Uh-huh, I thought so. He's got you by the balls, eh?

MAURICE:

No, it's not that. He just knows things. . . that no one
else knows.

21

CARMEN:

For Chrissake! If it's your screwing around, that's not gonna hurt you. Even I know about your little flings, Maurice—*all* of them. But that doesn't make me dangerous.

MAURICE:

I'm not talking about that. . . .

CARMEN:

You're not gonna tell me he's your bodyguard, are you? He's no bigger than a peanut.

MAURICE:

Carmen, there are things you don't know and it's better that you don't. Just sing and shut up. Close your eyes and plug your ears! That's all I ask!

CARMEN:

Well, it so happens I'm interested in Toothpick 'cause Toothpick interferes with my work. If he's your bodyguard or your mother, I couldn't care less, but when he sticks his feet in my spaghetti, then it's my business and I'm gonna scream.

MAURICE:

Why does he hate you so much? Why does he laugh at you? And why should he bother you this afternoon? He must have a reason.

Silence.

CARMEN:

You tell me why you're scared of him and I'll tell you why he's after me.

MAURICE:

You're asking for it. . . . Start prying up the lid, the whole thing might explode in your face.

CARMEN:
Let it explode here, not on stage.

MAURICE:
Okay. . . . Remember how Dum-Dum disappeared? And the big Brisebois? And Willy Ouellette with his Jew's harp who gave us all such a pain in the ass that they found him in an alley with two mouth organs jammed down his throat? Cobra, the serpent lady, who'd strangled one of her customers with her goddamned snake? And all the others in the seven years you've been with me? . . . You think I did all that by myself?

CARMEN:
Toothpick?

MAURICE:
That's right.

CARMEN:
But he's a puny turd. He's no bigger than a fence post.

MAURICE:
That's why he's so good. . . . He can go anywhere. He's got a good aim. And. . .lots of imagination.

CARMEN:
So. . .you put the finger on him, he puts it on you.

MAURICE:
Like it or not, we're in it together.

CARMEN:
Well. . .that explains a lot. But you're still gonna have to do something. Listen, Maurice. . .Toothpick is the *only thing* wrong with my life. . . . I'm a good singer and the show I'm doing tonight is professional like this joint has never seen. And the audience loves me. Which makes you rich. And I've realized that I've got things to say to those people because I love them, too. So I don't

want . . . you hear me . . . *I don't want* some two-bit killer sitting at the front table, burping in my face. If Toothpick is in this club tonight, it's your problem 'cause I won't set foot on stage. Have him go kill someone, lock him in the can, I don't care what, but make him disappear.

MAURICE:
You still haven't told me why he hates you.

CARMEN:
It's almost funny. He was plastered one night and he waited for me, here in my dressing room. He hid behind the screen. Oh, it wasn't that he wanted to sleep with me . . . . He wasn't the first . . . and he won't be the last . . . . But . . . 'cause he was plastered, he'd dropped his his pants. When I pulled back the screen, there he was, his pants on the floor . . . with his joint up . . . . But . . . he's got a tiny little dick and I must have laughed for ten minutes. Maybe he's good at killing people, but I doubt he can work miracles with what's between his legs. One thing's sure, if that's where he got his name, it fits him to a "T."

Silence.

One last thing I want to know. La Duchesse de Langeais, was that him too?

MAURICE:
Yes.

CARMEN:
Why did you do that? You knew I loved la Duchesse . . . .

HARELIP runs in.

24

HARELIP:
> Carmen...Maurice...I was outside the club with
> Sandra and Rose Beef...and I saw Gloria coming up
> the Main!

> *HARELIP exits.*

> *To the beat of a vigorous Argentine tango, GLORIA makes
> her entrance while the CHORUS follows her.*

CHORUS I:
> Gloria's coming!

CHORUS II:
> Gloria's coming!

CHORUS I:
> We haven't seen her for six months.

CHORUS II:
> At least six months!

ROSE BEEF:
> She's come to welcome Carmen....

SANDRA:
> You think so?

CHORUS I:
> Look how she's coming up the Main....

CHORUS II:
> Such a fallen monarch!

CHORUS I AND II:
> She's put on her last sequined brocades. Got out the last
> of her lace. Yet even in tatters, she has the air of an
> empress. Gloria-of-the-Port, covered with make-up and
> rags, has deigned to emerge from her hole to welcome
> the triumphant Carmen. Ah, when she struts by, I feel
> the samba tingle the length of my spine. Gloria-of-the-

25

Port bears with her the refrains of ailing tangos, of fractured Argentine tunes, the clack of castanets, the caress of flutes and harps. Gloria-of-the-Port transports the Mardi Gras of Rio in her walk and every gesture. But once she's passed by, it's as if there were a vacuum . . . as if Gloria had kept her entrancing music for herself. When Gloria looks at me, I'm a fireworks display. But when Gloria looks elsewhere . . . I'm nothing.

SANDRA:
Gloria is the music I liked yesterday.

CHORUS I AND II:
And she's never forgiven me for Carmen.

GLORIA: *to CARMEN*
You've come back, have you? I thought you were dead.

> *To MAURICE.*

Hello, gouger! You still scratching for lice? You still make your living off other people's vermin?

> *MAURICE exits.*

Did you see that, kid? Like a dog. You should have seen him twenty years ago. Me, I was Xavier Cugat and he was my chihuahua. When I was ashamed, I'd hide him . . . and when I wanted to make people laugh, I'd pull him out of my purse.

> *She laughs and takes a long look at CARMEN.*

Something tells me you haven't changed your style.

> *Silence.*

What do you do when you're ashamed of Maurice? A cowgirl doesn't have a purse. Do you hide him under your hat? But maybe he doesn't embarrass you.

Silence.

You got a cigarette, kid? South American music can't cover the cost any more.

CARMEN hands her a cigarette and lights it for her.

I won't say thanks, kid, 'cause whatever you've got today, you owe to me.

Silence.

This is the first time in ages I've been out of the house. Living over a garage on the waterfront isn't much fun, but it's less depressing than walking up a street that used to be great and now is ending her days as one long hot dog stand. When you and Maurice get home in the morning, don't you think your wig stinks of fried grease? Everything on the Main reeks of fat. . . . At least at my place, it smells of hops. Used to be when I'd look out our living room window, I'd see a rainbow of neon lights and the drunks would sing "La Cumparsita." Now from my window over the toilet, I can see the river . . . sometimes . . . .

Silence.

Six months ago, when I heard you were leaving, I thought you'd wised up and that you were gonna get . . . recycled, as they say. I said to myself: "She's finally gonna hang up her cowhides and her fake leather." But when I heard you were going to Nashville, boy, did I laugh! Nashville! Is that in Colorado at least? You know, you talked about Colorado in your songs so much, finally I figured it must be some street up in the north end of town. And did you finally meet a real horse, in person? I hope you weren't too scared. Did you sit on it for a picture so you'd have proof that at least you'd seen one?

There is a long silence.

GLORIA approaches CARMEN brusquely.

What have you done with everything I taught you, kid?
Don't turn away. Look at me...in the eyes. If I'd
known it was a clown I was hatching, I'd have stifled the
mother hen in me and smashed the egg with my beak.

Disgusted, she takes a few steps back.

So, did you practice your yodels in Colorado? Did you
transplant your vocal cords to your nose where they
belong? Now when you sing, is it your mouth or your
nose that moves?

GLORIA is on the verge of tears.

Nashville today, kid, is nothing compared to Miami
Beach in fifty-five. Have you ever been accompanied by
an orchestra of a hundred and one musicians? Have you
ever sung to a crowd of two thousand people on the
beach at dawn with the city of Miami Beach before you
and the Atlantic Ocean behind you? Have you ever sung
"La Paloma" in the biggest club in Florida, walking on
a bed of orchids that your fans have strewn on the
runway? Have you ever sung on a first class liner with
the passengers in long gowns and tails? Have you ever
sung with twenty-five Argentine dancers who carried
you on their shoulders and threw you in the air like you
were a bird of paradise? Have you ever descended from
the ceiling in a rain of balloons, confetti and streamers,
yelling Happy New Year to the entire world? Have you?

Silence.

Dignity, kid, is to get so you can talk about all that
without crying. I have yet to achieve dignity.

Silence.

I'll be in the audience tonight, kid. I'll do you that favour. And I'm the one who'll clap the loudest . . . and I'm the one who'll start the standing ovation. You'll have a standing ovation tonight, kid, and you'll owe it to me. Like everything else. And if people ask what I thought after the show, I'll tell them you've made great progress! You're fabulous! You've got a real feel for showbiz. I'll make sure you triumph tonight, kid, the better to crush you after. I've come to warn you, Gloria has decided to make her comeback. I've been talking about it so long, people think I'm all hot air . . . . But I've got this little pianist, see . . . . Ah! if you could see him, kid, he's only nineteen . . . he could have been my child . . . . He's nuts about South American music. He came to see me a while ago and he convinced me I should go back to work . . . . for the last five months, I've been working five hours a day, kid, and I'm fucking good! So watch out! I'm gonna start over . . . with a piano . . . and a mike . . . and a dress . . . And you watch me climb! The people of my generation haven't had time to forget my songs and kids today are sick of hearing about cowboys going around the mountain! That's okay, kid, you keep "throwing your lasso to the sky," but watch out you don't snag a jet plane bound for South America.

She heads towards the door.

You've never been nothing but an amateur, kid, but soon you're gonna kiss the ground before a real pro!

She goes out like a tornado, followed by her Argentine tango music.

CARMEN:
That someone you love should hate you so much . . . . I'd have liked to take her in my arms and tell her: "Gloria, I admire you. You know how much I admire you. And how grateful I am for all you've done for me . . . . And you know that I never wanted to take your place, not in Maurice's bed, nor at the Rodéo." But she wouldn't

have believed me. She is so convinced it's the contrary.
She thinks everyone else should be like her. For her,
there was never room for two. She taught me everything,
but she figured I'd wait till she died, then go on . . . doing
her. She wanted me to be just like her after she was
gone, so people would say as they watched me: "A real
Gloria! But the real Gloria was a lot better." All she
wanted was someone to take over. Whatever she did
wasn't really for me, it was for her own memory. She
thinks I'll do a bad show tonight, that she'll humiliate
me by clapping loud . . . . But it's her who'll be the flop
again, not me. Her too, she doesn't know what's in
store. Besides, she'll never understand that I don't care
about coming down from the ceiling in a shower of
balloons, singing in Spanish.

   HARELIP has entered while CARMEN was talking.

HARELIP:
  She's so pathetic . . . but it's her own fault! If you run
  after bad luck long enough, sooner or later you'll find it.

CARMEN:
  Has she left?

HARELIP:
  She went into Maurice's office.

CARMEN:
  Poor Maurice . . . thought he was rid of her for good.

HARELIP:
  She keeps popping up whenever she's had too much
  beer.

CARMEN:
  Amazing, eh? Spend your life on beer and never get fat.

30

HARELIP:

You know, I've seen her put longshoremen under the table when she was younger. Never gained an ounce... and she was never sick. Oh, it made her crazy, but never sick. But don't worry about her, she's not dangerous.

CARMEN:

What time is it?

HARELIP:

Forget the time. We'll start when we start.

CARMEN:

Have they begun to arrive?

HARELIP:

Yes.

CARMEN:

I'll go take a peek....

HARELIP:

No, no. Stay here and relax! Why don't you take off your wig, you must be hot.

CARMEN:

No, I'll keep it on....

HARELIP:

You put it on so early...and it only takes a second....

CARMEN:

I'm gonna keep everything on....Now that I'm ready, I want to stay ready....I'm not hot, Harelip, I'm just fine.

HARELIP:

How was practice?

CARMEN:
Good. The musicians down there were a lot better, but I was still glad to see the Rodéo guys again. Actually, you know, they're pretty good. Anyway...the music hasn't changed so much.... It's the words....

HARELIP:
I can't wait to hear it. Wow, songs that you wrote yourself! That must be fabulous! Must take a lot of brains too. It's not me who could do something like that!

Silence.

Carmen, are you gonna keep me as your dresser? I don't want to go back to the ladies room.

CARMEN:
Of course, I'm going to keep you. Like before.

HARELIP: *smiling*
You want me to massage your neck, like I used to.... You liked that....

CARMEN:
Good idea. What would I do without you, Harelip?

HARELIP goes to CARMEN and begins massaging her neck.

CHORUS I AND II:
They're standing in line outside the Rodéo.

CHORUS I:
That hasn't happened since the day Carmen left.

CHORUS II:
The other clubs are...

CHORUS I AND II:
...empty.

SANDRA:
Maurice even decided to close the Coconut.

HARELIP: *to CARMEN*
Relax now! Relax!

CHORUS I AND II,
SANDRA AND ROSE BEEF:
Everybody's there.

SANDRA:
Lola.

ROSE BEEF:
Mimi.

SANDRA:
Gerda.

ROSE BEEF:
Babalu.

CHORUS I AND II:
Miss Clairol.

HARELIP:
Relax.

CHORUS I AND II:
Katari Butch.

HARELIP:
You're not relaxed.

CHORUS I AND II,
SANDRA AND ROSE BEEF·
Bélinda.

CARMEN:
I'm relaxed.

CHORUS I AND II,
SANDRA AND ROSE BEEF:
  Roméo.

CARMEN:
  I'm relaxed.

CHORUS I AND II:
  The whole of the Main has turned out tonight.

CHORUS I:
  Even the pigs have come to see.

CHORUS I AND II,
SANDRA AND ROSE BEEF:
  The ringside is already full.

HARELIP:
  You've gotta let yourself go . . . . You can lean on me.

CHORUS I AND II,
SANDRA AND ROSE BEEF:
  Gloria is straight as a statue.

HARELIP:
  That's it.

CHORUS I AND II,
SANDRA AND ROSE BEEF:
  She can't keep her eyes off the dressing room door.

CARMEN:
  I feel so good when you do that to me.

HARELIP:
  That's it. . . . That's it . . . . That's it . . . . That's it . . . .

SANDRA AND ROSE BEEF:
  I managed to sneak right down to the edge of the stage.

SANDRA:
  Aie, stop pushing!

ROSE BEEF:
> Stop pushing!

CHORUS II:
> Stop pushing!

CHORUS I AND II:
> Stop pushing! Stop pushing!

ROSE BEEF:
> Look, even Maurice is nervous.

SANDRA:
> He's eyeing Toothpick in a strange way.

CHORUS I AND II:
> Toothpick was the first to arrive!

CHORUS I:
> He got the best table!

CHORUS II:
> And he ordered champagne!

CHORUS I AND II,
SANDRA AND ROSE BEEF:
> Doesn't say a word. He's waiting. For what?

> *Silence.*

CHORUS I AND II:
> Everybody's whispering.

> *Whispers are heard.*

CARMEN:
> Funny, I can't hear the house. . . .

CARMEN AND HARELIP:
> They're so quiet. Usually they scream. . . .

CARMEN:
They crack stupid jokes. . . .

HARELIP:
They run from table to table. . . .

Murmurs are heard.

CARMEN AND HARELIP:
They dance. . . . But tonight you can feel the tension everywhere. It's as if a storm were brewing!

The murmuring is more and more pronounced.

You could cut the electricity with a knife!

HARELIP:
I don't know why, Carmen, but suddenly I'm scared!

ROSE BEEF bursts out laughing.

CARMEN:
The first flash of lightning!

CHORUS I AND II,
SANDRA AND ROSE BEEF:
Carmen! Carmen!

HARELIP:
I'm scared!

CHORUS I AND II,
SANDRA AND ROSE BEEF:
Carmen!

HARELIP:
I'm scared!

CARMEN:
The first roll of thunder!

CHORUS I AND II,
SANDRA AND ROSE BEEF:
>   We want Carmen!

CARMEN:
>   The cloud has broken! My name is raining!

CHORUS I AND II,
SANDRA AND ROSE BEEF:
>   Carmen!

CARMEN:
>   Okay, Harelip, enough! I'm ready!

CHORUS I AND II,
SANDRA AND ROSE BEEF:
>   We want Carmen!

HARELIP:
>   I don't want you to go out!

CARMEN:
>   What?

CHORUS I AND II,
SANDRA AND ROSE BEEF:
>   Carmen!

HARELIP:
>   I'm scared!

CARMEN:
>   Why, that's crazy! Here goes. . . .

CHORUS I AND II,
SANDRA AND ROSE BEEF:
>   Tonight will be a big night!

HARELIP:
>   Be careful!

CHORUS I AND II,
SANDRA AND ROSE BEEF:
Tonight will be a big night!

CARMEN:
Don't worry.

CHORUS I AND II,
SANDRA AND ROSE BEEF:
Tonight will be a big night!

CARMEN:
I'm sure of what I'm doing!

Silence.

CARMEN moves towards the stage.

CHORUS I AND II,
SANDRA AND ROSE BEEF:
Carmen! Carmen! Carmen!

CARMEN:
Tonight will be a big night!

CHORUS I AND II,
SANDRA AND ROSE BEEF:
Carmen!

HARELIP:
Good luck. . . .

CHORUS I AND II,
SANDRA, ROSE BEEF AND HARELIP:
Carmen!

HARELIP:
I'll be watching from here. . . .

CARMEN: *with her back to the audience*
I've never seen the Rodéo so full. So bright! So
beautiful! My God! Toothpick! He's with Gloria!
Maurice couldn't keep him out. I'm not going! I'm
scared of him! I can't go out on stage! I can't! What
if. . .he laughs. . .with Gloria. . . . What if they've
planned it together! I've got to stop shaking! I've got to
stop!

CHORUS I AND II:
Carmen!

CARMEN:
I can't do it!

CHORUS I AND II:
Carmen!

CARMEN:
I can't do it!

      MAURICE runs in.

MAURICE:
Can I give Curly the signal?

      *CARMEN looks at MAURICE, panicstricken. There is
      a long silence.*

CARMEN:
Yeah, give him the signal.

      MAURICE exits.

      *Almost immediately, we hear the first chords of a Country
      and Western number which serves as the overture to
      CARMEN's show.*

The CHORUSES, SANDRA and ROSE BEEF
applaud, yelling and screaming.

During the overture, HARELIP speaks, while
CARMEN stands petrified, her back to the audience.

HARELIP:

They say that when Carmen was seven years old and it
was time to make her First Communion, her mother,
Marie-Louise, went to the finance company and
borrowed some money to buy a white dress, stockings,
shoes, a veil, a little purse and gloves. . . . And when
Carmen was all dressed, Marie-Louise told her right in
the middle of the store: "My God, you're ugly! A First
Communion girl is beautiful, but you, you're ugly. Are
you sure you're in a state of grace? You don't look in a
state of grace. Your eyes look funny. If you make your
First Communion and you're not in a state of grace, you
go straight to hell." They say that Carmen was so
frightened that she threw herself into her mother's arms,
crying: "I don't want to make my First Communion."

CARMEN AND HARELIP:

I can't!

HARELIP:

I'm not in a state of grace!

CARMEN AND HARELIP:

I don't want to go! Mama! Help me!

HARELIP:

They say that Marie-Louise gave the dress, the veil, the
stockings, the shoes, the gloves and the little purse back
to the saleslady and said she'd come back next year. But
Carmen made her First Communion that year anyway.
Instead of making it in the big ceremony with all the
other children, she got up at five o'clock that Sunday
morning and went to Communion alone, at the six
o'clock Mass, *before* all the others. The other children
weren't even dressed yet when Carmen was back in her

bed, asleep, with the taste of the wafer still in her throat
and one thought in her head: to get out of that
madhouse as fast as possible, so she could be rid of her
crazy mother. And that morning, in her dreams,
Carmen sang. That's what they say.

The overture is finished.

There is applause, screams and whistles.

CARMEN takes a deep breath.

CARMEN:
Mama! Help me!

She goes out on the stage of the Rodéo.

The CHORUSES stand and stare.

Blackout.

Act Two

TOOTHPICK slowly crosses the stage, a shotgun under his arm. He stops for a moment in the centre of the stage, as if to savour an important moment in his life, then he exits.

HARELIP enters.

HARELIP:
Carmen talked about me! In her songs, Carmen said things that come from my life! She told the story of me and Hélène . . . and she said it wasn't ugly. She even said it was beautiful! Carmen sang about how my life is beautiful and that me, Harelip . . . . How did she say it? . . . That I'm a love song asleep in a tavern! And Carmen said I could wake up someday! That if I'd wake up, then the Main would hear from me! Carmen said that deep down inside, I'm strong!

The two CHORUSES, led by SANDRA and ROSE BEEF, enter.

CHORUS I:
Wake up!

CHORUS II:
> Wake up!

CHORUS I:
> Get up!

CHORUS II:
> Get up!

CHORUS I AND II:
> Wake up! Get up! Get up! Get up!

HARELIP:
> People always told me I'm ugly. I'm vulgar. That I don't know how to talk! That I'm dirty!

CHORUS I:
> Don't just sit there!

CHORUS II:
> Don't just sit there!

CHORUS I AND II:
> Get up!

HARELIP:
> But Carmen told me that's not true.

SANDRA:
> Carmen talked about me! Carmen said things in her songs that come from my life.

ROSE BEEF:
> Carmen talked about me!

CHORUS I AND II:
> Wake up!

ROSE BEEF:
> Carmen said things in her songs that come from my life.

CHORUS I:
Get up!

CHORUS II:
Wake up!

SANDRA AND ROSE BEEF:
She told the story of me and . . .

SANDRA:
Carlo . . .

ROSE BEEF:
Baby Face . . .

SANDRA AND ROSE BEEF:
. . . and she didn't say it was ugly.

CHORUS AND HARELIP:
Carmen talked about me!

SANDRA AND ROSE BEEF:
She even said it was beautiful.

CHORUSES AND HARELIP:
Carmen said things in her songs that come from my life.

SANDRA AND ROSE BEEF:
Carmen said my life is beautiful and that me . . .

SANDRA:
Sandra . . .

ROSE BEEF:
Rose Beef . . .

SANDRA AND ROSE BEEF:
. . . I'm a love song asleep in a tavern.

CHORUSES AND HARELIP:
She sang about my life and she didn't say it was ugly.

SANDRA AND ROSE BEEF:
> And Carmen said I could wake up someday.

CHORUSES AND HARELIP:
> She even said it was beautiful.

SANDRA AND ROSE BEEF:
> And that if I'd wake up, then the Main would hear from me.

CHORUSES AND HARELIP:
> Carmen said my life is beautiful, that I'm a love song asleep in a tavern.

SANDRA AND ROSE BEEF:
> Carmen said that deep down inside, I'm strong!

CHORUSES AND HARELIP:
> Carmen said I could wake up someday.

SANDRA AND ROSE BEEF:
> Carmen said that deep down inside, I'm strong!

CHORUSES AND HARELIP:
> And that if I'd wake up, then the Main would hear from me.

ALL:
> Carmen said that deep down inside, I'm strong!

> *Silence.*

> Carmen said that deep down inside, I'm strong!

HARELIP:
> People always told me I'm ugly!

SANDRA:
> That I'm vulgar!

ROSE BEEF:
> That I don't know how to talk!

CHORUSES I AND II:
> That I'm dirty!

ALL:
> People were always ashamed of me! But Carmen told me I'm beautiful, that I can get out of the tavern!

> *Silence.*

> Out of the tavern!

CHORUS I:
> Wake up, she said!

CHORUS II:
> Get up, she said!

HARELIP, SANDRA AND ROSE BEEF:
> Don't just lie there!

ALL:
> Don't just sit there! Don't just sit there! I'll help you!

> *Silence.*

> Carmen said she'd help me! Ah! I'll never forget her last song!

> *CARMEN storms in, followed by MAURICE.*

MAURICE:
> When did you write that song?

CARMEN:
> Which one?

MAURICE:
> The last one! The last one!

CARMEN:
Same time as the others. . . .

MAURICE:
That's not an answer!

CARMEN:
What do you mean, it's not an answer?

MAURICE:
I want to know when! What day! And why!

CARMEN:
I don't know what difference the date makes. Why I
wrote it, that's something else. . . .

MAURICE:
You didn't sing that one when I went to get you in
Nashville. Was it already written or did you do it later?
That's what I want to know. I saw you in the car,
coming back. You spent days scribbling in that
goddamned notebook of yours! That's it, eh? You
thought you'd surprise me! In Nashville, all you sang
me were the little farts. You saved the big guns for
tonight!

CARMEN:
I barely had time in Nashville. By the end of the third
song, you were all over me, going on about how you'd
never heard such a singer.

MAURICE:
I was talking. . . about you, about the way you sing, the
way you take the stage, your voice. I wasn't talking
about your songs. . . . I was glad to see you hadn't gone
for nothing, that you were better than before.

CARMEN:
So, you didn't even listen. I could have sung that song
and you wouldn't have heard it!

MAURICE:
  That's a lie!

CARMEN:
  Come off it, you've always said if you've heard one
  Country and Western song, you've heard them all.
  Either you like Country and Western or you don't,
  there's no in between . . . and you don't like it, You never
  have. The only reason you ever let me sing it was 'cause
  you knew it would sell and with me you'd make money!
  Of course in those days, you were into South American
  fans and bananas on the head, which didn't quite pack
  the house, did it? Stop taking people for idiots,
  Maurice. We all know you're a weathervane that turns
  in the direction of the money. Well, let me tell you
  something, Mr. Silver-Dollar-Maurice, as for money,
  you never made half of what you've made tonight, not
  even in Gloria's finest hour.

MAURICE:
  Yeah, well it's not your new songs that made money
  tonight. It's because you're back. 'Cause you're a big
  star on the Main. You could have sung the same crap as
  before and there would have been just as many people
  out there.

CARMEN:
  Ah! So you admit what I sang tonight wasn't crap.

MAURICE:
  It was another kind of crap. Now, look, I sent you to
  Nashville so you could improve your technique. I sent
  you to Nashville to improve the technique of your
  yodel! Now all I ask is that you do a good yodel, you
  hear me? And what made me cry when I heard you
  down there was that you did a much better yodel. I've
  put time and money into your voice, Carmen, so your
  voice has got to pay off.

CARMEN:
  You can do more with a voice than yodel, Maurice.

MAURICE:
So I see!

CARMEN:
Did you hear them tonight, Maurice? Didn't you listen?
Have you ever seen them so wild? Do you think a few
yodels could make people cheer and whistle like that?
Do you think if I'd come back with the same kind of
lyrics, the crowd would have climbed on the tables and
chairs to keep me from leaving the stage? No one ever
got them to do that, Maurice, because no one's ever
talked to them. I didn't even realize it. For years, I've
been going on about the plains in Colorado and the
moon over Tennessee and my heartthrobs in Montana
and heroic Texans on white horses and adventures with
my lasso and my hammered-leather saddle shaped like
two ears and big black storm clouds and lovers up in
heaven and love that lasts forever! But I was cheating
them, Maurice. 'Cause that's not what they want to
hear. Sure, they did it when my voice wobbles around in
my throat, but did you hear what it does to them when
between the yodels I talk directly to them, about them,
and in their own words? Did you? Hell, people used to
sing my songs like parrots without a thought about what
they were saying. Now when they sing them, it's their
own lives they'll be singing about. Don't you think that's
wonderful? Yeah, I know, all you care about is money!
And I also know that things of the heart are not your
bag. Sentiment is not your department! So, fine, think
about the money, I'm not stopping you. My songs will
make you a fortune, Maurice, and you can start
counting it now. What's there to worry about? Sure,
people would have been there if I'd sung the old stuff
tonight, but what about tomorrow? And next week? I
tell you, there'll be as many tomorrow, maybe more,
'cause the Main needs someone to talk to it about the
Main. And if the Main'll come and listen to me talk to
her about herself, then she'll drink your lousy beer while
she's at it. So shut your mouth and ring up the cash!

50

MAURICE:

You damn fool! You don't realize what you've done tonight is dangerous.

CARMEN:

Ah-ha! There, the cat's out of the bag! You're scared of them!

MAURICE:

Right now, it's you I'm scared of. And believe it or not, I'm scared for you. You don't understand, what you're doing can blow up in your face.

CARMEN:

That's ridiculous!

MAURICE:

Oh, tonight was wonderful, they climbed on the tables and screamed that they loved you, and they'll be back tomorrow. It might last a month, six months, maybe a year. But what happens when they start doing what you've told 'em to do? Eh? Have you thought of that?

CARMEN:

I hope they do!

MAURICE:

Oh yeah? All right. Let's say they take your advice. Let's say they smarten up, they wake up and they get mad. Then what? It's fine to wake people up, but once they're awake, what do you do with them? I can tell you right now what they're gonna do, they're gonna head for the door. They're gonna split, that's all. And you'll be left standing there like a turkey on your big stage in your fancy outfit. You'll be singing to empty tables!

CARMEN:

Maurice, you don't understand. If they go, I go with them.

MAURICE:

Don't make me laugh! You think they'd take you along
dressed like that? And I know you well enough to know
you won't go singing in the streets! Which means you'll
stay here while they piss off somewhere else. 'Cause even
if they do wake up, and I know them, I know what
they're like, but even if they do, they'll go right back to
sleep for the first dude who'll give them a handout. And
all your big ideas about freedom turn into boozy
dreams. "Aie, man, you remember Carmen?" "Aie,
man, wasn't she something else, man?" Sure. But they'll
never come back to see you. They'll be too embarrassed.
So, you'll starve to death while the broad next door
makes a killing, 'cause she had the brains to just show
off her tits and sing, "Roll Out the Barrel." My poor
Carmen! You don't know them! You take old "Silver-
Dollar-Maurice's" word for it: people who end up on the
Main don't want to be saved. I've been working the
Main for twenty-five years, night and day, month after
month, year after year. The Main is my mother! She
brought me up. She gave me my first rap on the
knuckles, my first kick in the ass and my first dose.
There isn't a square inch of the Main that I don't know
by heart. And believe me, kiddo, it's not you who's
gonna change her. She's seen lots before you, and
tougher too, and she knew how to handle them. I can
tell you right now what'll happen and I don't want an
empty club on account of your bullshit!

CARMEN:

You never think of anyone but yourself, do you?

MAURICE:

You bet I don't!

CARMEN:

You say you know the Main by heart, yet you talk
about them like they were the scum of the earth. All you
care about is how much money you can suck out of
them.

52

MAURICE:

There's nothing else to do with them, Carmen, but to
make them spend their money. Can't you get that
through your head? Take a good look at them. Don't
you see who you sing for every night? Don't you see who
it is who thinks you're the best, most beautiful singer in
the world? Eh? A bunch of losers, drunks and junkies
who half the time don't even know where they are,
much less what they say, and who couldn't give a shit
about the songs you sing. Look, you know what I tell
the girls who start here? "You're a piece of ass, baby,
and don't forget it." Well, the same goes for you,
Carmen. You're a piece of ass around here too. So you
shook 'em up tonight, so you made 'em cry, that's real
nice and I'm real happy for you, but you're still just a
broad, Carmen. And once they're sick of hearing how
much you love them, they're gonna tell you to fuck off
and they'll ask for your old songs back. If you wake
them up, you'll only lose them, 'cause I tell you, they'll
split so they can go back to sleep somewhere else. And if
you don't wake them up, you'll just make a pain in the
ass of yourself and they'll still tell you to fuck off. So,
come on, get it through your thick skull, you're here for
entertainment, that's all. We're not the Salvation Army.
Your job is to dress up like a cowgirl, show off your legs,
get up on the stage, wiggle your ass and make them
drool by smelling strong and singing loud. It doesn't
matter what, but loud! Your talent is in your yodels,
sweetheart, and me, your boss, all I ask is that you be
the best around, the queen of the yodel, a babe who
brings in the customers, 'cause they'll have heard how
there's nobody else around with a set of pipes like yours.

He laughs.

"The Main needs someone to talk to it about the Main"?
The Main needs someone to give her a good screw!

CARMEN:
And if I want to keep trying my way?

MAURICE:

You won't try your way, 'cause tomorrow it's back to the oldies or you don't sing.

MAURICE starts to leave.

CARMEN:

Maurice. Listen for a minute. Tonight, while I was doing the song about Harelip, I was watching her. . . . Maurice, for Chrissake, she's your sister and she needs help!

MAURICE:

If anything could have been done with her, I'd have done it already.

CARMEN:

Oh, sure. And of course, you couldn't be wrong. Before I came here, all you'd let Harelip do was look after the ladies room, 'cause that's all you thought she was good for. But now she's learned to dress me, to take care of my clothes and my wigs. She's so proud of what she's doing, she watches over my dressing room like a Siamese cat with kittens. So, you were wrong that time, weren't you? How do you know it isn't the same for Rose Beef, for Sandra? What if it's not you they need, but me? What if I have a role to play in their lives? So they're junkies? Okay! So they're alkies? But who is it who gives them the dope? Who gets them drunk and leaves them to stew in their ignorance? It's us! You, with your money that's got to circulate, and me, with my talent that makes it circulate. You complain that the Main isn't what she used to be. . . . You bet she isn't! You never give her time to recuperate. You bleed her dry, then whatever you give her as a pick-me-up only poisons her more. You despise the Main 'cause she's dying, but you're the one who's killing her! But. . . I figure she's still got a chance. . . . Maurice, I've decided to use my voice to help the Main get out of its gutter. If I have to teach them how to breathe, I'll teach them how to breathe. . . . If I have to teach them everything, I'll

teach them all I know, even if that isn't much . . . . They
listen to me! They love me! And I love them! While I
was gone, I understood things, things that I want to try
to explain to them. They're down now, but they've got
to get back up. We haven't the right to leave them there.
I know I can help them to stand up, Maurice. What if
there is something they can do? What if it's not true that
I'm here just for entertainment? What if they really do
listen to me? Because the Main has been crawling in
filth ever since you've known her, is no reason to leave
her that way. What if, deep down inside, she wants to
change? For the better! What if she wants to be looking
down from up there, instead of looking up from down
here? What if she wants to walk a straight line along the
street, instead of staggering and bumping into store
windows? What if she wants to sing out and laugh,
instead of hugging the walls, beating her breast about
how it's her own fault if she's where she is now? What if
she wants to shout to the world: "Look, here I am! Here
I am!" Instead of whispering: "Forget about me, I'm
ugly!" What if she wants to be someone who's listened to
and respected, instead of being a tramp who gets raped
for twenty bucks at night, and during the day is ignored,
except when it's time to say how we're ashamed of her
and she doesn't deserve to live. The Main deserves to
live, but she needs help to realize it, to realize how! I
started tonight, Maurice, and I won't stop now. If you
want to help me, fine. If not, too bad. I feel strong
enough and sure enough to stand up to you. You know,
I could easily change from the best of your girls to the
worst of your enemies.

MAURICE:

You don't want to sing your old songs tomorrow, don't
come back. Go flog your stuff somewhere else.

Before leaving.

Take 'em down to Place Jacques-Cartier, see how long
you last!

MAURICE exits.

CARMEN:
>I'm right! I have to be right! It's impossible that people you love so much and who love you so much can just drop you and walk away. No. . . . No, I have to. . . . I have to keep them awake. It's up to me to keep them awake, to never let up; it's up to me to be good enough to keep them interested and to make them want to come back. That's it! They have to want to come back. That's what I have to make Maurice understand. He'll understand, I know he will. It's no big risk. Besides, it's not true they'll leave. And especially, it's not true they're scum. They act like scum when they're treated that way, but if you know how to talk to them, they're fine! No, if I drop them now, if I go back to my old songs tomorrow, then they'll leave! Then the joint will be empty! I can't sing about my phoney heartthrobs now, not after I've talked about their real problems. I haven't the right! I'm glad, because I can't turn back now. It doesn't matter what happens, I've got to keep going. I've got to go further! Isn't that great, there's no looking back. I've gone too far for that. And maybe the day will come when I won't have to dress up like a cowgirl and yodel. Maybe, little by little, I'll be able to shake off the Country and Western and find my own style! My own style! I started out with other people's words and music, but maybe one day, I'll have my own words and my own music. Yeah! To get up on stage and not feel. . .I have to disguise myself! Wow!

SANDRA:
>Can I see her?

ROSE BEEF:
>You think she'll let me go in?

HARELIP:
>I don't know. I don't think she's had time to change.

SANDRA:

Okay, never mind. I'll wait. I'll talk to her when she comes out.

ROSE BEEF:

I know she must be tired, but tell her I just want to give her a big kiss.

HARELIP:

Okay, I'll tell her. I'm sure it'll be okay. And I'm sure she'll join us for a beer, 'cause, this afternoon, she told me: "If it's a hit tonight, Harelip, I'll buy drinks for the whole gang."

CHORUS I AND II:

At the corner of the Main and la Catherine, I'm already describing what happened tonight to people who weren't there. I try to explain that the sun will be back again tomorrow, that the sun has come to stay, but I don't have the words. . . . I get all choked up. . . . I start to cry. For once, it's for joy! All of a sudden, Greta-the-Old, who's so good at imitations and who has an incredible memory, starts singing Carmen's last song, right in the middle of the street. Traffic stops. People look out their windows. Carmen's voice soars above the houses. Ah! It's as if. . . as if someone. . . someone were. . . washing me clean in a big waterfall!

CARMEN:

Tell them to come in.

HARELIP:

Are you sure?

CARMEN:

Sure, I'll change later.

HARELIP:

You can come in. Carmen's expecting you.

SANDRA and ROSE BEEF approach CARMEN.
They are silent and very impressed.

CHORUS I AND II:
> Greta-the-Old chokes on her yodels. Nobody laughs.
> "I'll just do the parts with words," she says. And she
> starts again.

CARMEN:
> Don't be embarrassed, it's only me.

ROSE BEEF:
> Oh, no. It's not only you. . . . For us, you're no longer
> the same.

CARMEN:
> Oh, come on! Ask Harelip! Eh, Harelip? I haven't
> changed, have I?

HARELIP:
> No, but they won't believe me. But you've got to
> understand them. When I saw you this afternoon, I was
> embarrassed too.

SANDRA:
> Don't worry, we'll get over it. We . . . we just want to say
> thank you, but we don't know how. We're not used to it.

CARMEN:
> You don't have to. I understood tonight at the end of the
> show. . . .

CHORUS I AND II:
> Greta-the-Old has finished. . . .

SANDRA:
> Did you see Gloria walk out?

CHORUS I:
> Someone yells:

CHORUS II:
"Encore!"

SANDRA:
She didn't look too happy. When she got up, it wasn't to clap, it was to get out!

CHORUS I AND II:
Greta-the-Old starts to sing for the third time. But she doesn't try to imitate Carmen any more. She sings with her own squawky old alcoholic voice.

ROSE BEEF:
Toothpick too!

CARMEN: *smiling*
My God! Toothpick! I forgot to talk to Maurice about him.

CHORUS I AND II:
One or two people start to sing with her. Then others. I sing too. Already, I know almost the whole song by heart.

ROSE BEEF:
After the last song, he slipped out like a rat.

HARELIP:
He's probably gone to get plastered again. Don't even think about him, Carmen, he's not worth it.

CHORUS I AND II:
Everyone's singing!

CARMEN:
You're right. Why should I care about him? Not tonight, anyway.

CHORUS I AND II:
Everyone's singing!

CARMEN:

> Okay, girls, I'm gonna change. Then, we all go for a drink.

CHORUS I AND II:

> Even the pigs. They're not too sure what they're singing, but they sing. It's as if time were suspended. I could sing like this till my dying day!

CARMEN:

> Five minutes, okay?

CHORUS I AND II:

> Till my dying day!

CARMEN:

> I want to take a shower.

> *A shotgun blast is heard from far off, like distant thunder.*

HARELIP, SANDRA AND ROSE BEEF:

> No!

CARMEN:

> I have to. . .to help me unwind.

HARELIP, SANDRA AND ROSE BEEF:

> Don't take a shower, Carmen. Don't go in there!

CARMEN:

> I need one. I'm all wound up.

HARELIP, SANDRA AND ROSE BEEF:

> Don't take a shower, Carmen. Don't go in there!

CARMEN:

> Why, just 'cause it's far from my dressing room? Don't worry, I won't catch cold.

CHORUS I AND II:

> People start to move on.

60

SANDRA:
>Stay as you are.

ROSE BEEF:
>Don't change.

HARELIP:
>Come like that.

>*CARMEN starts towards the exit. She is smiling.*

CHORUS I AND II:
>That's all very nice, but I've gotta go to work.

SANDRA:
>We want you in all your splendour!

HARELIP:
>Don't take your shower, Carmen!

ROSE BEEF:
>Come with us, right away!

CHORUS I AND II:
>Unless I take the night off.

HARELIP:
>There's no more soap!

SANDRA:
>There are no towels!

ROSE BEEF:
>There's no hot water!

>*They surround CARMEN, as if to protect her. A second shotgun blast is heard.*

CHORUS I AND II:
>That's it, I'll take the night off. We'll celebrate tonight.

HARELIP:
> You've got to come with us. . . .

SANDRA:
> Right away!

ROSE BEEF:
> Everyone's waiting for you!

CHORUS I AND II:
> Tonight, everyone celebrates!

HARELIP, SANDRA AND ROSE BEEF:
> Tonight, everyone celebrates!

HARELIP:
> Come on!

SANDRA:
> Quickly!

ROSE BEEF:
> Hurry up!

CHORUS I AND II:
> Tonight, everyone celebrates!

HARELIP, SANDRA AND ROSE BEEF:
> You've got to get out of here!

CARMEN:
> No. You go ahead. I'll join you later. I don't want to show off in my work clothes. It's not the star who'll have a beer with you, it's Carmen.

> *She exits.*

> *Silence.*

> *HARELIP, SANDRA and ROSE BEEF look at one another.*

HARELIP:
Go ahead, do like she said. I'll stay here, in case she needs me.

SANDRA AND ROSE BEEF:
You shouldn't have let her go.

HARELIP:
I know.

ROSE BEEF and SANDRA exit.

They say that on the day her parents died in a car crash, Carmen had come to see three shows at the Crystal. Three Westerns. And all the while she was watching the movies, Carmen felt that something important would happen that day, so they say. And coming out of the show, she came face to face with Gloria, who was the big star on the Main in those days. They say that Carmen said to Gloria: "Aren't you the one who sings in Spanish at the corner of la Gauchetière? Did you ever think of singing cowboy songs in French?" And Gloria answered: "Sorry, I don't speak French." On her way home that Saturday night, Carmen made up her mind to try to talk to her mother, to tell her she didn't want to keep working in a factory, that she wanted to be a singer. But when she got home, she learned that her mother, Marie-Louise, her father, Léopold, and her little brother, Roger, had all been killed in an accident on the boulevard Métropolitain. It was her sister, Manon, who had been given the news. They say that instead of breaking into tears, Carmen took Manon in her arms and cried: "It's a sign, Manon. It's a sign from heaven! Today is the day of our deliverance!"

CHORUS I AND II:
Today is the day of our deliverance!

Two shotgun blasts are heard.

HARELIP:
Yes, Carmen felt delivered, because now she knew there was nothing to stop her from becoming a singer. They say... they say, at her parents' funeral, Carmen looked like a bride.

HARELIP goes towards the exit.

I don't think Carmen should be alone.

She exits.

CHORUS I AND II:
Yes, I'll stay on the street to watch the sun come up, like yesterday. But this time, I'll be waiting for it. This time, I know it's going to rise... and I'll watch to see the sky grow light. But... the sky isn't light yet. It must still be too early. That's it, it's too early. I'll wait.... I may have to wait for it, but when it comes, watch out!

SANDRA:
I saw a light at the end of the street!

ROSE BEEF:
But it was lightning!

CHORUS I AND II:
The sky is clouding over!

HARELIP screams. Then, as if he'd been waiting to hear her scream, TOOTHPICK comes running on stage.

TOOTHPICK:
A terrible thing has happened. The most terrible thing possible. Don't look to the end of the street, it's no use. The sun won't come up any more.

SANDRA:
Why?

ROSE BEEF:
What's happened?

CHORUS I AND II:
Tell me!

*From the beginning of TOOTHPICK's monologue, the
lights grow weak and yellow, as if the CHORUSES were
fading out, little by little.*

TOOTHPICK:
I was there tonight at Carmen's show, you saw me. I
was sitting down front with Gloria. Oh, I thought
Carmen's show was a knockout too! Afterwards, I
couldn't even stay for the applause, I took off, 'cause. . .
'cause I didn't want people to see me cry. I ran out of the
club with Gloria. Out on the street, we threw ourselves
into one another's arms, saying we'd never heard
anything so beautiful. I took Gloria back to her place,
then I went home to bed. But I couldn't sleep. I kept
tossing around. . . . Finally, I decided to get up and go
see Carmen. I felt that I couldn't sleep until I had told
her how much she had moved me. I got dressed fast.
Just as I was leaving the house, I saw Sandra and Rose
Beef coming out of the club. I went in. . . not a sound. I
crossed the room and I went into Carmen's dressing
room. Nobody. I thought everyone had left. But all of a
sudden, I heard screaming at the other end of the
building. I recognized Carmen's voice. Then another
scream. It was Harelip. I ran into the hallway 'cause I
thought someone might be hiding in the club as a joke,
or maybe the girls had found a rat in the washroom, like
happened before. . . . But. . . I soon realized it was a
fight I was hearing. It was Carmen who was screaming
insults at Harelip, who was crying her eyes out. Oh, I
know what I'm telling you is horrible, but you must
know the truth. Ah, Carmen! If you could have seen
her. . . . Carmen was so ugly! Me, who'd come to tell
her I loved her, to express my admiration, I found
myself looking at someone in a rage, wrapped in a
towel, screaming, laughing, spitting. "You're as stupid

as the rest of them," she yelled, "you fell for it too and now you've got the nerve to make a pass at me. Do you think I'm interested in you, Harelip? After the success I've had tonight, you think I'm gonna fall into your arms and everything will be like before?" I couldn't believe my eyes. I stood crouched in the hallway. I wanted to rip my ears off so as not to hear, to rip my brains out so as not to understand. . . . Carmen. . . Carmen had always told us she was with Maurice, not Harelip. Carmen, a lesbian! I didn't want. . . I didn't want that. . . . Harelip was huddled in a corner, howling like a dog. "I fooled you all," Carmen said, "the whole gang. You fell for everything, hook, line and sinker. I suppose now you've got it in your heads there's a way out for you, eh? Ha! I never dreamed you'd buy it that fast! Well, so much the better! The faster I make my money, the faster I get out of here. What's the matter, Harelip? You look like a dead fish. Surprised, eh? Yes, I want out of here. You think I want to end up like Gloria, hang around for years, then wind up over a garage? I made contacts in the States, baby, and as soon as I've made a fortune singing to you suckers, I'm gonna blow this joint. I'm gonna disappear like a puff of smoke and you'll never see my lovely puss again!" Then, she started laughing like a maniac. "You should have seen your faces, tonight," she said. "The whole bunch of you looked so stupid. All you need is to have someone tell you you're beautiful, you're nice, especially that you're smart, and bingo, you imagine your lives have changed, life is beautiful and the Main is the cat's ass in a teacup. If the Main is the cat's ass, sweetheart, it's the cat's ass in the shit! And I've found my way out of it. Now get this, Harelip, starting next week, it's gonna cost double to come hear me tell you you'll get out. You're gonna cough up, you shitheads, you're gonna bleed yourselves dry to come hear me sing about how wonderful you are. I even hope you'll go into debt to hear me laugh in your faces. You'll never get out 'cause you're all sucks! And as for you, Harelip, I'm gonna take care of you first. . . . I put up with you 'cause I needed you to stay in Maurice's good grace. I let you touch me, feel me up, kiss me, even though you made me sick. But starting tomorrow, you're going back to the toilets!" Then Carmen undid her bath towel and walked up to Harelip, naked. "Take a good look," she whispered, "a last look...and see all you can, 'cause you'll never see me this way again." Then, she turned her back on Harelip and went into the shower.... The rest happened like lightning. I didn't have time to step in. I swear! I didn't have time! Harelip grabbed the shotgun that Maurice keeps hidden behind the rad in the washroom and....

CHORUS I AND II: *quietly*
Ah!

The lights go out completely on the CHORUSES. There is a long silence.

TOOTHPICK:
Harelip fired two shots into the shower. But you musn't blame her, you would have done the same thing.

Slowly, HARELIP enters. She is carrying a gun.

HARELIP:
When Carmen died, murdered by Toothpick, there was one little lesbian...helpless...who stood beside her.

TOOTHPICK:
Give me the gun, Harelip. We don't want anyone getting into trouble.

TOOTHPICK takes the gun and goes towards the door. He meets MAURICE.

I've done your dirty work again, Maurice. I hope you'll remember.

Before going out, he turns to the CHORUSES, which are now invisible.

TOOTHPICK:
>We're closing the club for a week. Starting next Monday, Gloria returns to her rightful place.

>*He exits.*

>*MAURICE and HARELIP stand face to face.*

MAURICE:
>If you put the finger on Toothpick, you put it on me.

>*Silence.*

>*In the midst of howls, hiccoughs, gurgles and inarticulate sounds, in a wash of feeble and anaemic South American music, beneath glaring lights of dubious taste, GLORIA appears on stage where CARMEN has just triumphed. Only her last two words are audible: "Mi coraçon."*

Orchestration of speeches for *Sainte-Carmen of the Main*:

	1.	2.	3.	4.	5.	6.	7.	8.	9.	10.	11.
CHORUS I:	They're standing in line outside the Rodéo.		The other clubs are...	empty.			Everybody's there.				
CHORUS II:	They're standing in line outside the Rodéo.			empty.			Everybody's there.				
SANDRA:		That hasn't happened since the day Carmen left.			Maurice even decided to close the Coconut.		Everybody's there.	Lola.			
ROSE BEEF:							Everybody's there.		Mimi.	Gerda.	
CARMEN:											Babalu.
HARELIP:						Relax now! Relax!					

	12.	13.	14.	15.
CHORUS I:	Miss Clairol.	Katari Butch.	Bélinda.	Roméo.
CHORUS II:	Miss Clairol.	Katari Butch.	Bélinda.	Roméo.
SANDRA:			Bélinda.	Roméo.
ROSE BEEF:			Bélinda.	Roméo.
CARMEN:			I'm relaxed.	I'm relaxed.
HARELIP:	Relax.	You're not relaxed.		

	16.	17.	18.	19.	20.
CHORUS I:		Even the pigs have come to see.	The whole of the Main has turned out tonight.		Gloria is straight as a statue.
CHORUS II:			The whole of the Main has turned out tonight.		Gloria is straight as a statue.
SANDRA:					Gloria is straight as a statue.
ROSE BEEF:					Gloria is straight as a statue.
CARMEN:				You can lean on me.	
HARELIP:			You've gotta let yourself go . . .		

71

21.

CHORUS I:	She can't keep her eyes off the dressing room door.
CHORUS II:	She can't keep her eyes off the dressing room door.
SANDRA:	She can't keep her eyes off the dressing room door.
ROSE BEEF:	She can't keep her eyes off the dressing room door.
CARMEN:	I feel so good when you do that to me.
HARELIP:	That's it . . . . That's it . . . . That's it . . . . That's it . . . .

22.

CHORUS I:	
CHORUS II:	
SANDRA:	I managed to sneak right down to the edge of the stage.
ROSE BEEF:	I managed to sneak right down to the edge of the stage.
CARMEN:	
HARELIP:	

23. Aie, stop pushing!

24. Stop pushing!

25.

CHORUS I:	Stop pushing!
CHORUS II:	Stop pushing! Stop pushing!
SANDRA:	
ROSE BEEF:	
CARMEN:	
HARELIP:	

26. Look, even Maurice is nervous.

27.   28.

CHORUS I: Toothpick was the first to arrive.
CHORUS II: Toothpick was the first to arrive.
SANDRA: He's eyeing Toothpick in a strange way.
ROSE BEEF:
CARMEN:
HARELIP:

29.   30.   31.

CHORUS I: Doesn't say a word. He's waiting. For what?
CHORUS II: Doesn't say a word. He's waiting. For what?
SANDRA: Doesn't say a word. He's waiting. For what?
ROSE BEEF: And he ordered champagne. Doesn't say a word. He's waiting. For what?
CARMEN:
HARELIP: He got the best table!

32.   33.   34.

CHORUS I: *Silence.* Everybody's whispering. *Whispers.*
CHORUS II: *Silence.* Everybody's whispering. *Whispers.*
SANDRA: *Silence.*   *Whispers.*
ROSE BEEF: *Silence.*   *Whispers.*
CARMEN:
HARELIP: Funny, I can't hear the house.....

35.

CHORUS I:	
CHORUS II:	
SANDRA:	
ROSE BEEF:	
CARMEN:	They're so quiet. Usually they scream,
HARELIP:	They're so quiet. Usually they scream.

36.

CHORUS I:	*Whispers.*
CHORUS II:	*Whispers.*
SANDRA:	*Whispers.*
ROSE BEEF:	*Whispers.*
CARMEN:	crack stupid jokes.
HARELIP:	

37.

CHORUS I:	
CHORUS II:	
SANDRA:	
ROSE BEEF:	
CARMEN:	They dance....
HARELIP:	They run from table to table. They dance....

38.

CHORUS I:	*Murmurs.*
CHORUS II:	*Murmurs.*
SANDRA:	*Murmurs.*
ROSE BEEF:	*Murmurs.*
CARMEN:	But tonight, you can feel the tension everywhere.
HARELIP:	But tonight, you can feel the tension everywhere.

39.

CHORUS I:	*Murmurs.*
CHORUS II:	*Murmurs.*
SANDRA:	*Murmurs.*
ROSE BEEF:	*Murmurs.*
CARMEN:	It's as if a storm were brewing! You could cut....
HARELIP:	It's as if a storm were brewing! You could cut....

40.

CHORUS I:	*Murmurs are more and more pronounced.*
CHORUS II:	*Murmurs are more and more pronounced.*
SANDRA:	*Murmurs are more and more pronounced.*
ROSE BEEF:	*Murmurs are more and more pronounced.*
CARMEN:	the electricity with a knife.
HARELIP:	the electricity with a knife.

41.

CHORUS I:
CHORUS II:
SANDRA:
ROSE BEEF: *ROSE BEEF bursts out laughing.*
CARMEN:
HARELIP: I don't know why, Carmen, but suddenly I'm scared!

42.

43.

CHORUS I: Carmen! Carmen! Carmen!
CHORUS II: Carmen! Carmen! Carmen!
SANDRA: Carmen! Carmen! Carmen!
ROSE BEEF: Carmen! Carmen! Carmen!
CARMEN: The first flash of lightning!
HARELIP: I'm scared! I'm scared!

44.

45.

The first roll of thunder!

46.

CHORUS I: We want Carmen! Carmen!
CHORUS II: We want Carmen! Carmen!
SANDRA: We want Carmen! Carmen!
ROSE BEEF: We want Carmen! Carmen!
CARMEN: The cloud has broken! My name is raining!
HARELIP:

47.

48.

75

49.

CARMEN: Okay, Harelip, enough! I'm ready!

50.

CHORUS I: We want Carmen!
CHORUS II: We want Carmen!
SANDRA: We want Carmen!
ROSE BEEF: We want Carmen!
HARELIP: I don't want you to go out!

51.

CARMEN: What?

52.

CHORUS I: Carmen!
CHORUS II: Carmen!
SANDRA: Carmen!
ROSE BEEF: Carmen!
CARMEN: I'm scared!

53.

HARELIP: Why, that's crazy!

54.

CHORUS I: Tonight will be a big night!
CHORUS II: Tonight will be a big night!
SANDRA: Tonight will be a big night!
ROSE BEEF: Tonight will be a big night!
CARMEN: Here goes. . . .
HARELIP: Be careful!

55.

CHORUS I: Tonight will be a big night!
CHORUS II: Tonight will be a big night!
SANDRA: Tonight will be a big night!
ROSE BEEF: Tonight will be a big night!
CARMEN: Don't worry.

56.

CHORUS I: Tonight will be a big night! Carmen! Carmen! Carmen!
CHORUS II: Tonight will be a big night! Carmen! Carmen! Carmen!
SANDRA: Tonight will be a big night! Carmen! Carmen! Carmen!
ROSE BEEF: Tonight will be a big night! Carmen! Carmen! Carmen!
HARELIP: I'm sure of what I'm doing!

57.

CHORUS I: *Silence.*
CHORUS II: *Silence.*
SANDRA: *Silence.*
ROSE BEEF: *Silence.*
CARMEN: *Silence.*
HARELIP: *Silence.*

58.

CARMEN: Tonight will be a big night!

59.

CHORUS I: Carmen!
CHORUS II: Carmen!
SANDRA: Carmen!
ROSE BEEF: Carmen!

60.

HARELIP: Good luck....

61.

CHORUS I: Carmen!
CHORUS II: Carmen!
SANDRA: Carmen!
ROSE BEEF: Carmen!
HARELIP: I'll be watching from here....

TALONBOOKS — PLAYS IN PRINT 1981

Colours in the Dark - James Reaney
The Ecstasy of Rita Joe - George Ryga
Captives of the Faceless Drummer - George Ryga
Crabdance - Beverley Simons
Listen to the Wind - James Reaney
Esker Mike & His Wife, Agiluk - Herschel Hardin
Sunrise on Sarah - George Ryga
Walsh - Sharon Pollock
The Factory Lab Anthology - Connie Brissenden, ed.
Battering Ram - David Freeman
Hosanna - Michel Tremblay
Les Belles Soeurs - Michel Tremblay
API 2967 - Robert Gurik
You're Gonna Be Alright Jamie Boy - David Freeman
Bethune - Rod Langley
Preparing - Beverley Simons
Forever Yours Marie-Lou - Michel Tremblay
En Pièces Détachées - Michel Tremblay
Lulu Street - Ann Henry
Three Plays by Eric Nicol - Eric Nicol
Fifteen Miles of Broken Glass - Tom Hendry
Bonjour, là, Bonjour - Michel Tremblay
Jacob's Wake - Michael Cook
On the Job - David Fennario
Sqrieux-de-Dieu - Betty Lambert
Some Angry Summer Songs - John Herbert
The Execution - Marie-Claire Blais
Tiln & Other Plays - Michael Cook
The Great Wave of Civilization - Herschel Hardin
La Duchesse de Langeais & Other Plays - Michel Tremblay
Have - Julius Hay
Cruel Tears - Ken Mitchell and Humphrey & the Dumptrucks
Ploughmen of the Glacier - George Ryga
Nothing to Lose - David Fennario
Les Canadiens - Rick Salutin
Seven Hours to Sundown - George Ryga
Can You See Me Yet? - Timothy Findley
Two Plays - George Woodcock
Ashes - David Rudkin
Spratt - Joe Wiesenfeld
Walls - Christian Bruyere
Boiler Room Suite - Rex Deverell
Angel City, Curse of the Starving Class & Other Plays - Sam Shepard
Buried Child & Other Plays - Sam Shepard
The Primary English Class - Israel Horovitz
Mackerel - Israel Horovitz
Jitters - David French
Balconville - David Fennario
Aléola - Gaëtan Charlebois
After Abraham - Ron Chudley
Sainte-Marie Among the Hurons - James W. Nichol

The Lionel Touch - George Hulme
The Twilight Dinner & Other Plays - Lennox Brown
Sainte-Carmen of the Main - Michel Tremblay
Damnée Manon, Sacrée Sandra - Michel Tremblay
The Impromptu of Outremont - Michel Tremblay

TALONBOOKS — THEATRE FOR THE YOUNG

Raft Baby - Dennis Foon
The Windigo - Dennis Foon
Heracles - Dennis Foon
A Chain of Words - Irene N. Watts
Apple Butter - James Reaney
Geography Match - James Reaney
Names and Nicknames - James Reaney
Ignoramus - James Reaney
A Teacher's Guide to Theatre for Young People - Jane Howard Baker
A Mirror of Our Dreams - Joyce Doolittle and Zina Barnieh